# ADIA

Words and Music by SARAH McLACHLAN
and PIERRE MARCHAND

**Wistfully**

# SARAH McLACHLAN
## for piano solo

Photo courtesy Photofest

ISBN 978-1-4584-7163-5

HAL•LEONARD®
CORPORATION
7777 W. BLUEMOUND RD. P.O. BOX 13819 MILWAUKEE, WI 53213

Visit Hal Leonard Online at
**www.halleonard.com**

*mf*   *più mosso*

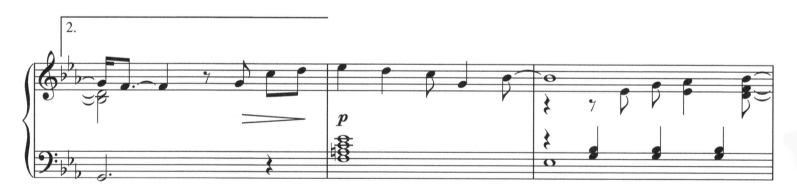

# ANGEL

Words and Music by
SARAH McLACHLAN

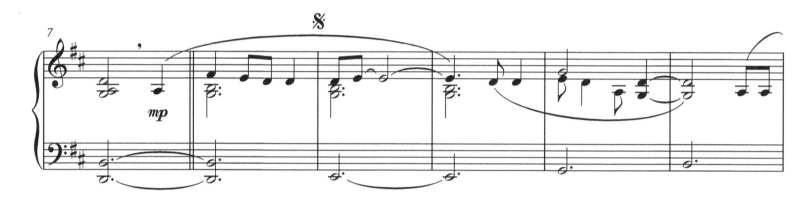

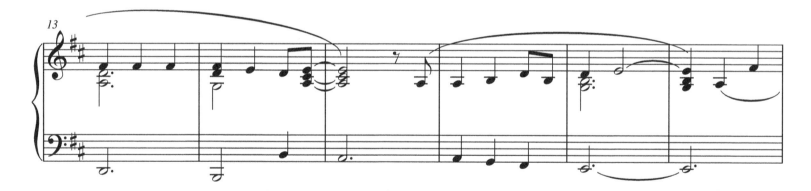

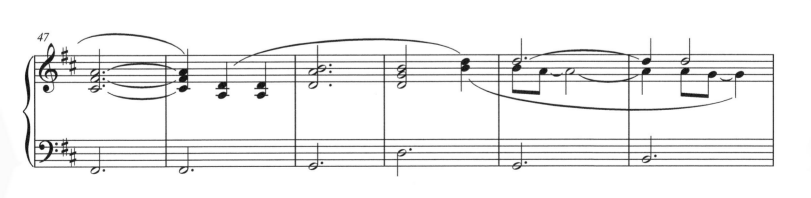

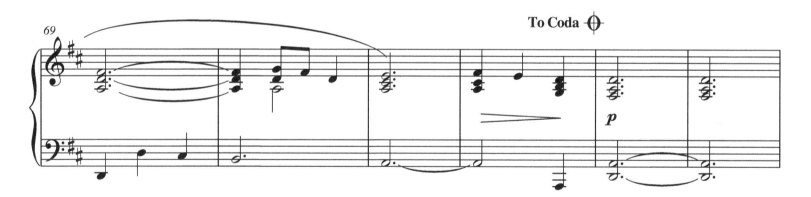

**CODA**

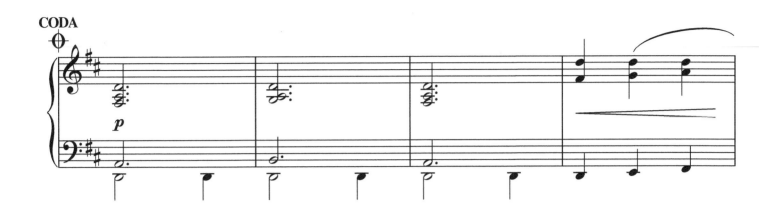

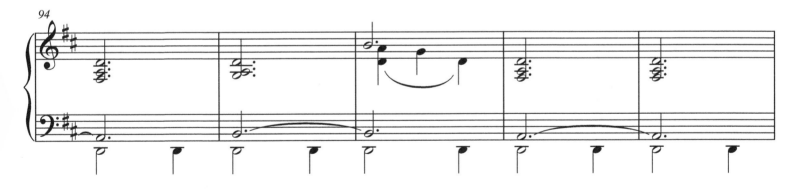

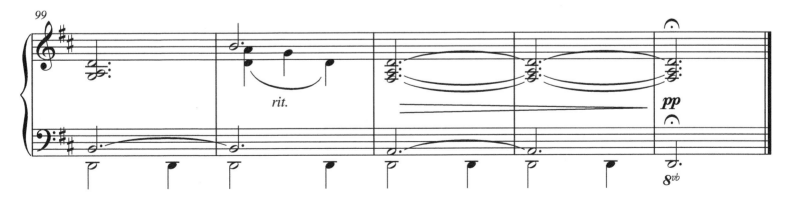

# BUILDING A MYSTERY

Words and Music by SARAH McLACHLAN
and PIERRE MARCHAND

**At a relaxed tempo**

# FALLEN

Words and Music by
SARAH McLACHLAN

# GOOD ENOUGH

Words and Music by
SARAH McLACHLAN

**Ballad**

22

# I WILL REMEMBER YOU

### Theme from THE BROTHERS McMULLEN

Words and Music by SARAH McLACHLAN,
SEAMUS EGAN and DAVE MERENDA

**Moderately**

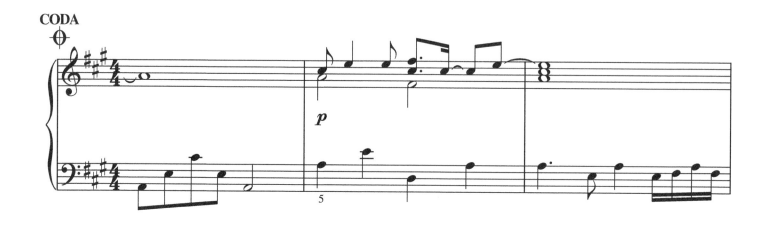

# ICE CREAM

Words and Music by
SARAH McLACHLAN

# INTO THE FIRE

Words and Music by SARAH McLACHLAN
and PIERRE MARCHAND

**With movement**

# STUPID

Words and Music by
SARAH McLACHLAN

**Flowing, with a pulse**

# SWEET SURRENDER

Words and Music by
SARAH McLACHLAN

**Moderate Soft Rock**

**To Coda** ⊕

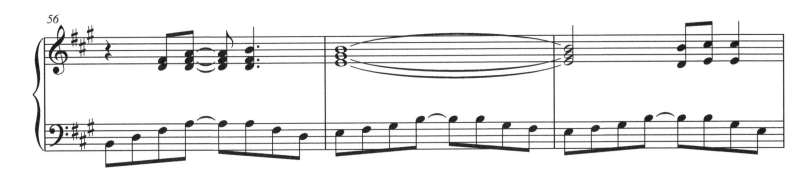

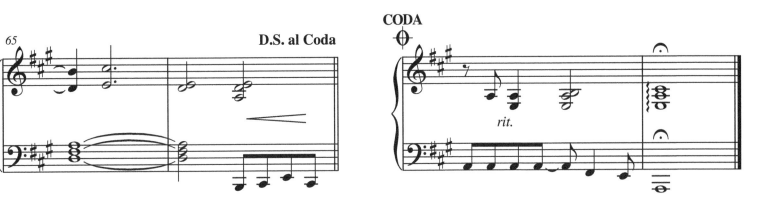

# WORLD ON FIRE

Words and Music by SARAH McLACHLAN
and PIERRE MARCHAND

**Relaxed groove**

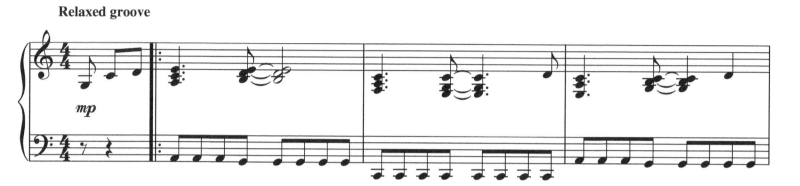

# VOX

Words and Music by
SARAH McLACHLAN

**Light Pop-Rock feel**

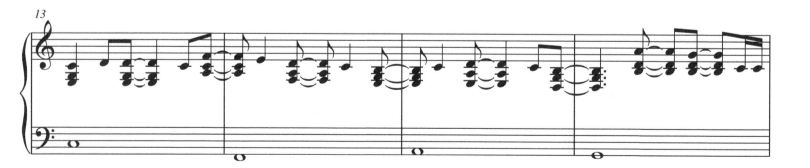